COMMUNICATION
THEN AND NOW

by Robin Nelson

first step nonfiction

Lerner Publications · Minneapolis

Communication is sharing ideas and news.

Communication has
changed over time.

Long ago, people made
pictures to tell stories.

Now, people write words
to tell stories.

5

Long ago, people copied
each book by hand.

Now, people use a **printing press** to print lots of books.

Long ago, people tapped
messages on a **telegraph**.

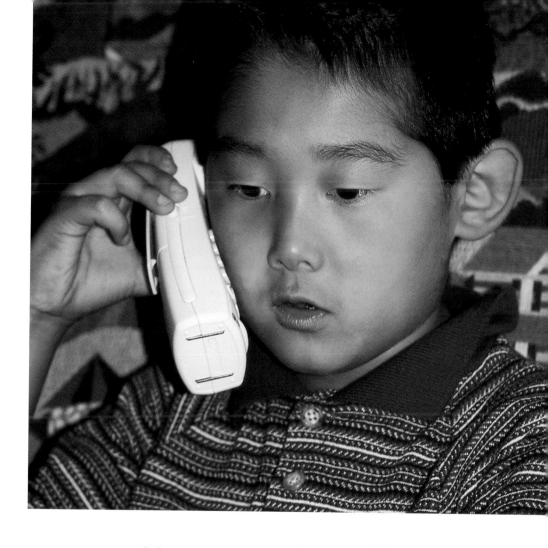

Now, people call on
a telephone.

Long ago, people wrote
letters.

Now, people write e-mails on a computer.

NEW YORK. MONDAY, JULY 8, 1889.

PR

Average Movement of Prices.

The bull market of 1885 began July 2, with the average price of 12 active stocks 61.49.

The rise culminated May 18, 1887, with the same twelve stocks selling at 93.27.

Prices gradually declined for about a year, reaching the next extreme low point April 2, 1888, the 12 stocks selling at 5.28. The movement since then, counting from one turning point to another, follows:

last low point	Apr. 2, 1888,		75.28
allied to	May 1,	"	83.54
eclined to	June 13.	"	77.12
allied to	Aug. 8,	"	85.95
eclined to	Aug. 18.	"	83.76
allied to	Oct. 1.	"	88.10
eclined to	Dec. 5.	"	81.88
allied to	Feb. 18, 1889,		87.77
eclined to	Mar. 18.	"	83.59
allied to	June 12.	"	91.38
losed Sat. night	July 6,	"	87.71

The Market To-Day.

There is some reason for believing that operators identified with the bear party sent early orders to London to depress mericans in that market as a preparation for the opening ere. These orders were faithfully executed, and London at 30 was quoted as opening weak and as having become very eak. Prices, however, were only a little below New York losinff figures.

London houses were, however, sellers at the opening, and here developed a decided lack of buyers. Lake Shore furished an illussration. It opened at 101¾ and was then offered own an eighth at a time to 101 where the next sale was made. his temper started a rush to sell out, during the first hour, rices generally went off from ¼ to 1½. In St. Paul Mr. Randolph had a large selling order; in Union Pacific Mr. avin made the lowest prices. Reading was sold by Oppeneim & Co., by Mr. Burras and Mr. Wheeler, and Northwest vent down on sales by Davis Johnson. Traders made most of he transactions in Atchison although there was evidence of ome support when the other market was weakest. The Trust tocks were not a feature. although weakening in sympathy

Clearings Last Week.

Boston special—The Post's table of clearings shows gross exchanges of 41 cities for the week ending July 6, 1889, $1,127,114,523, against $883,993,314 last year, an inc. of 27.5%. Outside of New York the inc. is 14.2%. New York inc. 37.3%, Boston 27.9, Philadelphia 6.3, St. Louis, 33.6, San Francisco 18, Cincinnati 7.2, Kansas City 27.5, New Orleans 3.1, St. Paul 2, Omaha 39.5, Minneapolis 15.2, Detroit 2, Denver 70.5, Peoria 12.7, Indianapolis 3.9, Ft. Worth 90.3, Wichita 48.4, Chicago dec. 5%, Milwaukee 1.6, Duluth 44.6 and Topeka 4.9.

For the month of June exchanges of 40 cities show an increase of 22.2%. Outside of New York increase 9.3%. New York increase 30.3%, Boston 18.8%, Philadelphia 12.1%, Chicago 0.1%, St. Louis 18.9%, San Francisco 2.7%, Kansas City 0.4%, St. Paul 2.1%, Omaha 20.8%, Denver 26.6%, Peoria 23.8%, Ft. Worth 47%, Topeka 18.4%. Duluth decrease 45.5%.

For 6 months gross exchanges of 40 cities show an increase of 15.8%. Outside of New York increase 11.9%. New York increase 18.2%, Boston 11.8%, Philadelphia 15.9%, Chicago 7.8%, St. Louis 8.5%, San Francisco 1.9%, Kansas City 11.3%, Omaha 19.5%, Denver 38.9%, Peoria 17.3%, Duluth 13.6%, Ft. Worth 31.8%, Topeka 31.4%.

Bankers Exerting Their Power.

Chicago special—It is stated on excellent authority that the Western presidents are getting positive orders from New York and Boston banking houses to settle the Western troubles at the meeting to-morrow. Some sort of plan to take care of C., B. & N. will be considered, and it is believed that if C., B. & N. can be controled, a general settlement will be effected.

Sales of stocks from 12 to 1—Listed 47,426; unlisted 5,454. Total, listed 194,408; unlisted 27,866.

12.40 p. m.—Slayback sold Union Pacific down.

The first bale of cotton from the South was sold at auction in front of the Cotton Exchange to-day and was bought by Henry Clews & Co. at 16¼.

Press. Cincinnati—It is reported here from a reliable source that Sullivan and Kilrain were fighting at 11.45 a.m. The contest was a long one and Sullivan was having the best of it and was sure to won.

1.35—Van Emburgh sold 2,000 Missouri Pacific.

The Position of Alton.

Long ago, newspapers brought news to hundreds of people.

Now, newspapers bring news
to millions of people.

Long ago, people could only
listen to news on the radio.

Now, we can watch news on television.

Long ago, the **pony express** took news across the country.

Now, the **Internet** carries news around the world.

Communication Timeline

1436
Printing press invented.

1837
Electric telegraph invented.

1876
Telephone invented.

1784
First U.S. daily newspaper published.

1860
The pony express began.

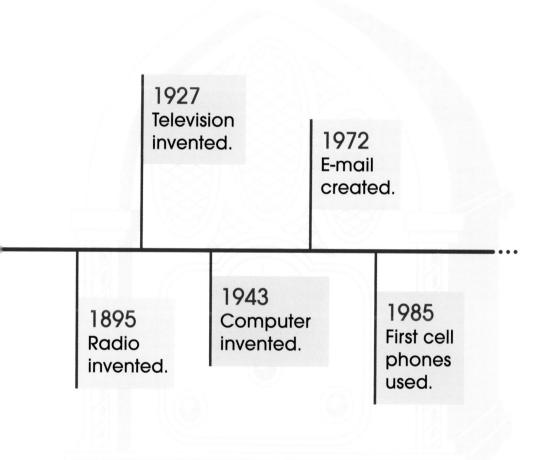

1927
Television
invented.

1972
E-mail
created.

1895
Radio
invented.

1943
Computer
invented.

1985
First cell
phones
used.

...

Communication Facts

 About 99% of homes in the United States have at least one radio.

 Today a computer can store one million times more information than the first computer. Today's computers are also 50,000 times faster.

 The telephone is the most-used piece of communication equipment in the world.

The first words spoken on a telephone were "Come here, Watson. I want you." This was the inventor Alexander Graham Bell calling his helper.

 The first television picture was a straight line.

 The first computer was 80 feet long. It weighed 30 tons.

Glossary

 communication – sharing thoughts, information, and news

 Internet – many computers that are connected and that communicate with each other

 pony express – a way to carry mail on horseback, used in 1860 and 1861

 printing press – a machine that prints books by pressing paper onto ink

telegraph – a machine that sends messages by wire or radio

Index

Internet – 17

newspapers – 12, 13

pony express – 16

printing press – 7

radio – 14

telegraph – 8

telephone – 9

television – 15

Copyright © 2003 by Robin Nelson

All rights reserved. International copyright secured. No part of this book may be reproduced, stored in a retrieval system, or transmitted in any form or by any means—electronic, mechanical, photocopying, recording, or otherwise—without the prior written permission of Lerner Publishing Group, Inc., except for the inclusion of brief quotations in an acknowledged review.

The photographs in this book are reproduced through the courtesy of: © Minnesota Historical Society, front cover, pp. 3, 8, 22 (bottom); © Stockbyte, pp. 2, 22 (top); © John D. Cunningham/Visuals Unlimited, p. 4; © Diane Meyer, pp. 5, 17, 22 (second from top); © Erich Lessing/Art Resource, NY, p. 6; © Martin Black/SuperStock, pp. 7, 22 (second from bottom); © Jack Ballard/Visuals Unlimited, p. 9; © Underwood Photo Archives/SuperStock, p. 10; © Photodisc Royalty-Free, p. 11; Dow Jones & Company, p. 12; Los Angeles Times, p. 13; © Brown Brothers, p. 14; © Lisette Le Bon/SuperStock, p. 15; © CORBIS, pp. 16, 22 (middle).

Lerner Publications Company
A division of Lerner Publishing Group, Inc.
241 First Avenue North
Minneapolis, MN 55401 USA

For reading levels and more information, look up this title at www.lernerbooks.com.

Library of Congress Cataloging-in-Publication Data

Nelson, Robin, 1971–
    Communication then and now / by Robin L. Nelson.
        p.   cm. — (First step nonfiction)
    Includes index.
    ISBN-13: 978-0-8225-4638-2 (lib. bdg. : alk. paper)
    ISBN-10: 0-8225-4638-8 (lib. bdg. : alk. paper)
    1. Communication—United States—History—Juvenile literature. I. Title. II. Series.
    P92.U5 N45 2003
    302.2'0973—dc21   2002010682

Manufactured in the United States of America
13-47603-4655-4/9/2019